Sports Trivia Quiz

Lagoon Books, London

Editor: Heather Dickson
Author: David Lever
Illustrator: Michael Grimsdale
Additional contributors: Sheila Harding,
Peter Kirkham, Rosie Atkins
Page design and layout: Linley Clode
Cover design: Gary Inwood Studios

Published by:
LAGOON BOOKS
PO BOX 311, KT2 5QW, UK

ISBN: 1899712267

Printed in France.

Sports Trivia
Quiz

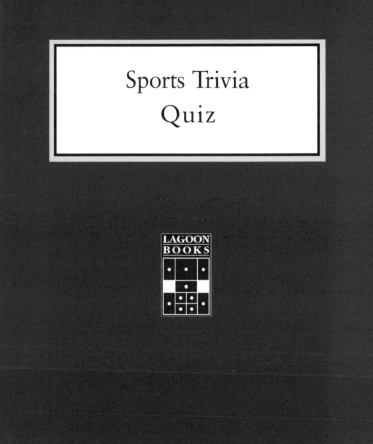

LAGOON
BOOKS

Other titles available from Lagoon Books

Introduction

At last a sports quiz which even the keenest of sportsmen and most dedicated armchair fans will find challenging. With every imaginable type of question on almost every sport, from soccer to tennis and golf to basketball, ski-ing to athletics and motor racing to baseball, this pocket-sized book is an absolute winner!

While some questions test your memory - forcing you to cast your mind back to the 1978 soccer World Cup final, the 1988 Calgary Olympics and the 1992 Wimbledon finals; others test your general knowledge. You may know how many players there are in a water polo side, but do you know which sportsman starred as Oddjob in the James Bond movie Goldfinger or in which sport you might pull taffy, move the pile and grind it out?

Designed to give even the top trivia brains a good work out, this quiz will provide hours of competitive fun, whether read alone, or played as a group.

What is the link between all of these?

1   Equestrian high jump

2   3,000 metre team race

3   200 metre hurdles

4   4,000 metre steeplechase

5   Standing long jump

6   Stone throw

7   Two-handed javelin throw

8   56 lb weight throw

In which sporting films do the following appear?

Harold Abrahams ①

Rocky Balboa ②

Pelé ③

Jake La Motta ④

Aldaniti ⑤

Fast Eddie Felson ⑥

Ben Hogan ⑦

Rocky Graziano ⑧

Name the sport associated with each of these positions

1. Tight end

2. Prop

3. Fine leg

4. Anchor leg

5. Crumbs gatherer

6. Short stop

7. Mollberg

8. Superman

What do these pairs have in common?

Ben Johnson and Hans Gunnar Liljenvall **(1)**

Wilma Rudolph and Ray Ewry **(2)**

Roger Brousse and Mike Tyson **(3)**

Bob Beamon and Jonathan Edwards **(4)**

Epee and Sabre **(5)**

Greg Rusedski and Lennox Lewis **(6)**

Zola Budd and Juan Rodriguez **(7)**

Portsider and southpaw **(8)**

In which one sport might you do all the following?

1. Pull taffy

2. Muff

3. Move the pile

4. Grind it out

5. Flood the zone

6. Strip the ball

7. Ring the bell

8. Split the uprights

In which game or sport would you use each of the following?

(1) A broom

(2) A mallet

(3) A piton

(4) Seven huskies

(5) A spider

(6) A spinnaker

(7) A castle

(8) A spooned blade

How many...?

Hoops are there in a croquet set (1)

Umpires in a cricket test match (2)

Players in a water polo side (3)

Pockets in three cushion billiards (4)

Players in an Australian rules
football side on the pitch at one time (5)

Balls are given to the umpires
before a baseball game (6)

Laps in the Indianapolis 500 (7)

Faults for knocking down a fence
in a show jumping competition (8)

How much...?

1. Does a men's shot weigh in athletics

2. Was Mike Tyson fined for biting the ear of his opponent Evander Holyfield

3. Did Fred Perry's tennis racket fetch at auction in 1997

4. Was the maximum British soccer player's wage until 1960

5. Is a middleweight boxer's weight limit

6. Is the sequence red, blue, red, yellow worth in snooker

7. Did Chris Taylor, the heaviest wrestler in Olympic history, weigh when he won bronze in 1972

8. Weight did cricketer Dean Jones lose in his eight-hour innings in Madras in 1986

Solve the cryptic clues to obtain the sporting answer

Two gymnastic drunks, directly
opposite each other, on
which apparatus?
(1)

If you're a Fosbury flop you will lose
your job in this field event
(2)

See poor Yorick and his reflection
whilst rowing
(3)

What a fencer would wrap a chicken in?
(4)

The longest diurnal lepidopterous
insect in the pool
(5)

Robert Sledge and Robert Sledge in
the Winter Olympics
(6)

Hurl a useful tool of the trade
across the field
(7)

Glide over the numbers on ice
(8)

In which one sport might you do any of the following?

(1) Throw some heat

(2) Go around the horn

(3) Choke up

(4) Hit a bleeder

(5) Hit a blooper

(6) Throw a duster

(7) Have a rhubarb

(8) Hit the dirt

What colour(s) are associated with the following?

Detroit Lions

Gary Player

12th Dan in judo

Dutch soccer shirts

The five Olympic rings

Grand Prix flag indicating
'slow down and hold position'

Tour de France's king of the
mountain jersey

The Boston Red Sox's socks

What are their real Christian names?

1. Tommy Nakajima

2. Too Tall Jones

3. Magic Johnson

4. Babe Ruth

5. Fuzzy Zoeller

6. Butch Wilkins

7. Buster Douglas

8. Keke Rosberg

What sports do you associate with the following celebrities?

1   Bing Crosby

2   Elton John

3   Richard Branson

4   Paul Newman

5   Peter O'Toole

6   Prince Charles

7   Cliff Richard

8   Omar Sharif

What sports compete for the following trophies?

Harry Vardon Trophy **(1)**

Webb Ellis Cup **(2)**

FIFA World Cup **(3)**

Stanley Cup **(4)**

MacRobertson International Shield **(5)**

America's Cup **(6)**

Heisman Trophy **(7)**

Val Barker Cup **(8)**

What was won by the following?

(1) Victor Diez y Diez in the Narcea River

(2) Yang Yang in 1989

(3) Hans Stuck in Germany and Switzerland in 1934

(4) Santa Claus at Epsom in 1964

(5) The Sheen Farmers in 1980

(6) Sinjin Smith and Randy Stoklos at Ipanema Beach, 1987

(7) John Ngugi five times between 1986 and 1992

(8) Rich Wonders in 1982

Where would you find all of these?

Wankel ①

Con rod ②

Boost ③

Bore ④

Crankcase ⑤

Drag coefficient ⑥

Normal aspiration ⑦

Venturi ducts ⑧

Who was the first...?

1 Black swimmer to win an Olympic gold medal

2 Woman to play men's pro basketball

3 Olympic athlete to fail a sex chromosome test

4 German to win the Wimbledon Men's Singles Championship

5 Czech to win the Wimbledon Ladies' Singles Championship

6 Man to swim the English Channel from shore to shore

7 American to win the World Chess Championship

8 Rower to win four successive Olympic gold medals

What are, or were, their real names?

The Ebony Antelope (1)

The Golden Bear (2)

FloJo (3)

The Kaiser (4)

The Refrigerator (5)

The Pampas Bull (6)

Joe Willie White Shoes (7)

Nasty (8)

What are the following?

1. Kendo

2. Pétanque

3. Pelota

4. Fives (Eton)

5. Drag racing

6. Hurling

7. Tae kwon do

8. Bandy

How long...?

(1) Is a circuit at Le Mans

(2) Is a swimming pool used for short-course competitions

(3) Is the Kentucky Derby

(4) Was Bob Beamon's Long Jump at the Mexico Olympics in 1968

(5) Is the maximum length of a Polo pitch

(6) Was it before another Olympic Games took place after 1936

(7) Is a hold-down, worth Waza-ari, in judo

(8) Is the Oxford v Cambridge Boat Race

In which year did...?

Yugoslavia win the men's basketball Olympic gold

Brazil get to keep the Jules Rimet Trophy

The New York Mets first win the World Series

Roger Bannister break the four minute mile

Cassius Clay win an Olympic gold

Pat Cash win the Men's Singles Championship at Wimbledon

Olga Korbut win Olympic gold on the beam and floor

Arnold Palmer first win the US Masters

What is, or was, their sport?

1. Bhagwant Chandrasekhar

2. Pedro Delgado

3. Yankee Express

4. Jockey Wilson

5. Hamilton Academicals

6. Beat Bunzli

7. Calgary Flames

8. Metaloplastika Sabac

What do these initials stand for?

NBA MVP (1)

MCC (2)

IOC (3)

CIPS (4)

US NLTA (5)

BBBC (6)

IIHF (7)

FIA (8)

What are these early forms of games now known as?

1   Pok-ta-Pok

2   Jeu de Mail

3   Baggataway

4   Sphairistike

5   Kalv

6   Qui Wan

7   Mintonette

8   Chaturanga

Who are described here along-side their other occupations?

1984 Olympic gold medal weightlifter and millionaire tuna fisherman **(1)**

England international soccer player and plumber **(2)**

1970s and 1980s cricketer and gravedigger **(3)**

Formula One champion and special police constable **(4)**

Kenyan 1968 1,500 metre Olympic gold medallist and Nandi tribesman **(5)**

Finnish 5,000 and 10,000 metre Olympic gold medallist in 1972 and 1976, and policeman **(6)**

1952 3,000 metre Olympic steeple-chaser and FBI agent **(7)**

Freestyle Olympic gold medalist in 1924 and 1928, and actor **(8)**

Name the sports star who appeared in each of these films

1 As the American footballer in Airplane

2 As himself in Space Jam

3 As the tennis player in Octopussy

4 As Oddjob in Goldfinger

5 As the major role in Enter The Dragon

6 As the decathlete in Can't Stop the Music

7 Toting a gun in Freedom Road

8 As the title role in Flash Gordon

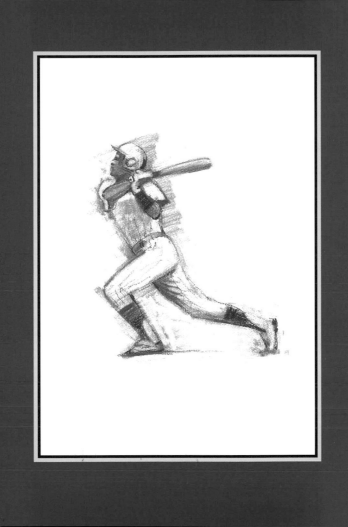

What are all of these?

1. Pinehurst

2. Firestone

3. Southport and Ainsdale

4. Eldorado

5. Greenbriar

6. Winged Foot

7. Thunderbird

8. Wannsee

Are they male or female?

Valeriy Borzov and Valeriy Brumel **1**

Kerry Saxby and Kerry Reid **2**

Pat Eddery and Pat Todd **3**

Toni Hewitt and Toni Starin **4**

Shane Gould and Shane Warne **5**

Kim Men-nam and Kim So-Young **6**

Ossi Reichart and Ossie Ardiles **7**

Lilian Camberabero and Lillian Board **8**

Who are the following? All the surnames begin with B.

(1) He won seven consecutive pole vault World Championship titles

(2) He won five consecutive Wimbledon Men's Singles Championships

(3) He was the first European golfer to win the US Masters

(4) He was the first man to hold all four Grand Slam tennis titles simultaneously

(5) He won the 100 metre title at the 1996 Olympic Games

(6) She won the women's singles at the US Tennis Championships three times in the 1960s

(7) She won three Olympic 500 metre speed skating titles

(8) He was the first black African to win an Olympic gold in athletics

Who are the sports personalities in these anagrams?

Join Al, charmed (basketball)

Broke scribe (tennis)

Aid cocaine man (gymnastics)

Event oiler (golf)

Pink oike (running)

No dear, I am a god (football)

Drive heavenly fold (boxing)

To want player (American football)

What do all of these have in common?

(1) Watkins Glen

(2) Clermont-Ferrand

(3) Zandvoort

(4) Nivelles

(5) Avus

(6) Anderstorp

(7) Brooklands

(8) Paul Ricard

In which sport would you see each of the following?

A night watchman **(1)**

A bandit **(2)**

A knuckler **(3)**

A crampit **(4)**

A quiver **(5)**

A kitty **(6)**

An eskimo roll **(7)**

A seramade **(8)**

How high are each of the following?

(1) The crossbar in American football

(2) A badminton net at the centre

(3) A tennis net at the centre

(4) A soccer goal crossbar

(5) A baseball pitcher's mound

(6) A netball ring and net

(7) An Olympic highboard diving platform

(8) A table tennis net

At what age did...?

1. Juan Manuel Fangio win the Grand Prix World Championship in 1957

2. Norman Whiteside first appear in a soccer World Cup tournament

3. Mike Tyson first win the World Heavyweight title

4. Lester Piggott win the Derby in 1954

5. Sonja Henie first participate in the Olympics

6. Sir Eyre Massey Shaw win the Olympic yachting gold medal in 1900

7. Martina Hingis win the Ladies' Singles Championship at Wimbledon

8. Michael Chang become the youngest-ever male tennis player to win a Grand Slam event

What else do these sporting pairs have in common?

Olympic swimmers Buster Crabbe and Herman Brix **(1)**

Soccer stalwarts Alf Ramsey and Stanley Matthews **(2)**

Golfers Severiano Ballesteros and Tom Kite **(3)**

Wimbledon tennis champions John McEnroe and Jimmy Connors **(4)**

Baseball's Babe Ruth and Hank Aaron **(5)**

Gold winning decathletes William Toomey and Nikolai Avilov **(6)**

Jump jockeys Brian Fletcher and Tommy Stack **(7)**

Formula One champions Jim Clark and Emerson Fittipaldi **(8)**

In which one sport will you find all of these?

1   Pope

2   Bolt and hair rigs

3   Roach

4   Barbel

5   Pinkies

6   Squatts

7   Terminal tackle

8   Hook disgorger

Name the countries where these soccer teams play

Colo Colo

Hazard Utd

Flamengo

Dong Thap

Norma

Stationary Stores

Canon Yaounde

Vital'O

How many...?

1 Metres in a marathon

2 Perfect scores of 10 did Nadia Comaneci achieve at the 1976 Montreal Olympics

3 Gold medals did Mark Spitz win at the 1972 Munich Olympics

4 Goals did Geoff Hurst score during the 1966 World Cup Soccer Tournament

5 Medals did Russia win at the 1984 Los Angeles Olympics

6 National teams take part in Baseball's World Series

7 Hurdles in a 110 metre hurdles race

8 Love letters did Katarina Witt receive after the 1984 Winter Olympics Figure Skating Competition

Which one event has at some time been associated with...?

Courchevel

Morzine

Marennes

Pac

Disneyland

Alpe d'Huez

Forges les Eaux

Champs-Elysées

Name the sport featured in each of these movies

1 Horse Feathers

2 Cool Runnings

3 The Mighty Ducks

4 Viva Las Vegas

5 Space Jam

6 Superargo

7 Caddyshack

8 Hard, Fast and Beautiful

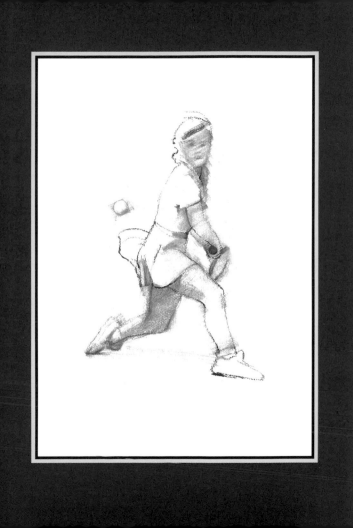

In which one sport might you do all the following?

(1) Cherry-pick

(2) Garbage

(3) Glass ball

(4) Double pump

(5) Cripple

(6) Alley-oop

(7) Slough off

(8) Get white man's disease

Name the sport associated with these terms

A reverse sandwich **(1)**

A bonk bag **(2)**

A jerk **(3)**

Spring the jack **(4)**

A Danish swipe **(5)**

A schussboomer **(6)**

A face-off spot **(7)**

A dumper **(8)**

What is their nationality?

(1) Clay Regazzoni (Formula One)

(2) Michael Lynagh (Rugby Union)

(3) Ilie Nastase (Tennis)

(4) Liselotte Neumann (Golf)

(5) Naural El Moutawakel
(400 metre hurdles)

(6) Jansher Khan (Squash)

(7) Ivan Mauger (Speedway)

(8) Edwin Moses (400 metre hurdles)

How many...?

Penalty shoot-outs did the German soccer team lose between 1976-1996 **1**

Calypso songs have been written about Olympic sprinter Hasely Crawford **2**

Miles/kilometres in the Marathon Des Sables **3**

Dimples on a golf ball **4**

Times did Eddie Mercx win the Tour de France **5**

Times have the Summer Olympic Games been held in the USA **6**

Miles/kilometres in the Decatriathlon **7**

Feathers on a shuttlecock **8**

What sport features in the following books?

1 Life at the Limit, by Professor Sid Watkins

2 Through the Covers, by Christopher Lee

3 Fever Pitch, by Nick Hornby

4 To Jerusalem and Back, by Simon Kelner

5 This Bloody Mary, by Jonathan Rendall

6 Living the Dream, by Hakeem Olajuwon

7 Too Soon to Panic, by Gordon Forbes

8 Final Rounds, by James Dodson

In which sport will you find these principles or rules?

The principle of verticality **(1)**

Only the backward and out frog-leg is allowed **(2)**

Repeated lifting will result in disqualification **(3)**

Match penalty if any injury results from spearing or butt-ending **(4)**

Dew is not a loose impediment **(5)**

Stones must reach the far hog line, but go no further than the back line, to be in play **(6)**

Exclusion foul for splashing in the face of an opponent intentionally **(7)**

Automatic disqualification for using a helmet (not worn) as a weapon **(8)**

Name the authors who wrote the following?

1 Soccer is *"a species of fighting"*

2 *"My writing is nothing, my boxing is everything"*

3 *"Pam, I adore you, Pam, you great big mountainous sports girl"*

4 *"Everybody ought to play golf, and nobody can begin too soon"*

5 *"'You skate, of course, Winkle ?' said Wardle"*

6 *"'What's Tangent doin' in this race?' said Lady Circumference"*

7 *"It is the first time that ever I heard breaking of ribs was sport for ladies"*

8 *"None but true anglers feel that gush of joy - That flushes in the patient minds employ"*

Who said the following?

(1) *"If my IQ had been two points lower, I'd have been a plant somewhere"*

(2) *"At Rangers I was third choice left-back behind an amputee and a Catholic"*

(3) *"Your hands can't hit what your eyes can't see"*

(4) *"You just press the accelerator to the floor and steer left"*

(5) *"If people don't want to come to the ballpark, nobody's going to stop them"*

(6) *"I ain't never liked violence"*

(7) *"If you're playing against a friend who has big boobs, bring her to the net and make her hit backhand volleys"*

(8) *"My greatest strength is that I have no weaknesses"*

Which sporting personalities are described here?

A vaulting vicar who won Olympic gold in 1952 **(1)**

He threw up over the winner of the 10,000 metres at the 1920 Antwerp Olympics **(2)**

A Liverpool soccer goalkeeper who injured his shoulder ironing **(3)**

A pole vaulter who invented the toy called The Erector Set **(4)**

He played drums for James Brown and won an Olympic boxing gold in 1976 **(5)**

They raised gloved clenched fists on the podium at the 1968 Mexico Olympics **(6)**

She won 1984 Olympic gold in the pool, and dislocated her knee modelling shoes **(7)**

He is the founder of the modern Olympic movement **(8)**

What are their married names?

1. Chris Evert

2. Mary Decker

3. Evonne Goolagong

4. Florence Griffith

5. Billie Jean Moffitt

6. Barbel Eckert

7. Debra Flintoff

8. Jacqueline Joyner

Where are these venues and what takes place there?

Croke Park ①

Stade Roland Garros ②

The Crucible Theatre ③

Wrigley Field ④

Flushing Meadow ⑤

MCG ⑥

Hubert H. Humphrey Metrodome ⑦

Badminton Park ⑧

What was the year of the first...?

(1) Super Bowl

(2) Soccer World Cup Final

(3) Modern Olympics

(4) Tour de France

(5) Baseball World Series

(6) Indianapolis 500

(7) Oxford v Cambridge Rugby Union match

(8) Wimbledon Lawn Tennis Championship

What sport do you associate with each of these films?

North Dallas Forty **(1)**

When We Were Kings **(2)**

Gregory's Girl **(3)**

White Men Can't Jump **(4)**

Bull Durham **(5)**

Kingpin **(6)**

This Sporting Life **(7)**

Slap Shot **(8)**

What sports do these teams play?

1. Beobanka Belgrade

2. Manchester Storm

3. Hunter Mariners

4. Casino

5. New York Yankees

6. Sydney Swans

7. Frankfurt Galaxy

8. Sheffield Wednesday

Which ball has the greater mass?

1 Table tennis or squash

2 Soccer or rugby

3 Tennis or golf

4 Hockey or tennis

5 Golf or squash

6 Cricket or baseball

7 Soccer or volleyball

8 Cricket or hockey

What do the following sportsmen have in common?

The American light-heavyweight boxing champion James Scott **(1)**

British 400 metre runner David Jenkins **(2)**

French cyclist Eric Ramelot **(3)**

British jockey Lester Piggott **(4)**

Former world heavyweight boxing champion Sonny Liston **(5)**

American 100 metre and 4x100 metre relay Olympic gold medallist Bob Hayes **(6)**

England and Arsenal soccer player Tony Adams **(7)**

Argentinian soccer star Diego Maradona **(8)**

Where...?

(1) Did baseball's Brooklyn Dodgers move to

(2) Was the 1991 USPGA Golf Championship held

(3) Were the 1992 Olympic Games held

(4) Was the 1997 Ryder Cup played

(5) Is the Orange Bowl

(6) Will you find Bears, Cubs and Bulls

(7) Were the 1934 and 1990 World Cup Soccer finals held

(8) Was the first modern Olympic competition held

Name the...

Identical twins that won the synchronised swimming duet gold in 1992

Player that André Agassi beat in the 1992 Wimbledon final

British ski-jumper who came last at the 1988 Calgary Olympics

French motor racing driver known as the Professor

Sport played by Pavel Bure, Jaromir Jagr and Alexei Yashin

Apparatus on which you might see moves named Thomas or Yamashita

Game in which 300 is the perfect score

Sport originally known as Poona

Who...?

1) Is allowed to shoot for goal in netball

2) Might shout yoshi

3) Might wally jump

4) Is the basketball player who wrote 'Walk on the Wild Side'

5) Might you find in a planche

6) Threw 22 completed passes in the 1993 Super Bowl

7) In the 1992 Olympic 4,000 metre individual pursuit final won gold and was the first cyclist to catch his opponent

8) Quit basketball in 1993 to join the Birmingham Barons baseball team

In which sport might you...?

Have a penholder grip on the paddle (1)

High five a setter after a successful smash (2)

Balk after losing your binding (3)

Shave-down ready for negative splits (4)

Hit the tin going for a drop (5)

Go in-off with too much screw (6)

Try a neck-mare before the single-leg Boston crab (7)

Use a tiller and a boom (8)

Which is the odd pairing, and why?

1. Gary and Phil Neville (Soccer)

2. Ralf and Michael Schumacher (Motor racing)

3. Michael and Leon Spinks (Boxing)

4. Mark and Steve Waugh (Cricket)

5. Rory and Tony Underwood (Rugby Union)

6. Martin and Graham Bell (Downhill ski racing)

7. Graham and Damon Hill (Motor racing)

8. Patrick and John McEnroe (Tennis)

What banned substances led to their disqualification?

1. Diego Maradona, soccer, banned in 1991, 1994 and 1997

2. Bill Werbeniuk, snooker, suspended 1988

3. The Chinese volleyball team, 1992 Olympics

4. Sweden's pentathlon team, 1968 Olympics

5. Ben Johnson, 100 metres, 1988 Olympics

6. Nijole Medvedieva, long jump, 1992 Olympics

7. The Polish ice hockey team, 1988 Olympics

8. Alexander Watson, modern pentathlon, 1988 Olympics

Where...?

Will you find Falcons, Hawks and Knights **(1**

Will the 2004 Olympics be held **(2**

Will the 2002 soccer World Cup be held **(3**

Were the first Olympic Games held after the Second World War **(4**

Are sight screens positioned in cricket **(5**

Did Muhammad Ali light the Olympic flame **(6**

Were the first Pan-American games held **(7**

Did Brazil win the Jules Rimet Trophy outright after winning it for the third time **(8**

Who won and what was the score?

(1) USA v Soviet Union, 1972 Olympic basketball final

(2) Argentina v Holland, 1978 soccer World Cup final

(3) Oakland 'A's v San Francisco Giants, 1989 World Series baseball

(4) The timeless ten day test match, England v South Africa, 1939

(5) Dallas Cowboys v Pittsburgh Steelers, 1996 Super Bowl

(6) St Kilda v Melbourne, Australian rules football, 6 May 1978

(7) Sampras v Agassi, US Open final, 1990

(8) New Zealand v Japan, rugby union, 1 November 1987

Who are the sportsmen hiding in these anagrams?

Go get beers (Soccer) **(1)**

Nat dealt him rice (Indy and Motor racing) **(2)**

Wires to God (Golf) **(3)**

Steam papers (Tennis) **(4)**

Bloody vain Ena (Sprinting) **(5)**

Deliver gas (Sprinting) **(6)**

Makes yer dry-clean (Athletics) **(7)**

Final deliveries (Cricket) **(8)**

Which sport do the following compete in?

1. Alex Criville

2. John Kocinski

3. Nobuatsu Aoki

4. Max Biaggi

5. Aaron Slight

6. Luca Cadalora

7. Carl Fogarty

8. Michael Doohan

Name the year that...

Nigel Mansell won the Brazilian Grand Prix and Andre Agassi won Wimbledon **(1)**

Gary Player won the US Masters Golf and West Germany won the FIFA World Cup **(2)**

Pittsburgh Steelers won the Superbowl and Martina Navratilova won the Women's Singles at Wimbledon for the second time **(3)**

Brazil won the Jules Rimet Trophy and Arnold Palmer won the British Open Golf Championship **(4)**

Manchester United won the Premier League and Irish swimmer Michelle Smith struck gold in Atlanta **(5)**

Sebastian Coe and Steve Ovett won gold in Moscow and the Philadelphia Phillies won the Baseball World Series **(6)**

USSR were Ice Hockey World Champions and Scotland and France shared the Rugby Union Five Nations Championship **(7)**

Bobby Charlton made his 100th appearance for England's soccer team and Tony Jacklin became the first Briton in more than 50 years to win the US Open Golf Championship **(8)**

Where were the Summer Olympics held in these years?

1   1900

2   1920

3   1932

4   1956

5   1960

6   1964

7   1980

8   1992

Where are these famous race courses?

(1) The Curragh

(2) Longchamps

(3) Happy Valley

(4) Woodbine

(5) Aintree

(6) Randwick

(7) Churchill Downs

(8) Musselburgh

At which race circuits would you find these famous corners...?

Mirabeau  **(1)**

Rivazza **(2)**

Becketts **(3)**

Sachs Curve **(4)**

Eau Rouge **(5)**

Spoon Curve **(6)**

Corkscrew **(7)**

Pinneirinho **(8)**

In which country would you find the following ski resorts?

1. Jackson Hole

2. Borovets

3. Taos

4. Turoa

5. Tignes

6. Whistler

7. Aviemore

8. Thredbo

What sporting event links the following places?

Cape Town - South Africa (1)

Fremantle - Australia (2)

Fort Lauderdale - USA (3)

La Rochelle - France (4)

São Sebastião - Brazil (5)

Sydney - Australia (6)

Baltimore - USA (7)

Auckland - New Zealand (8)

Solutions

Q1 They are all discontinued Olympic events

Q2 1) Chariots of Fire 2) Rocky 3) Escape to Victory
4) Raging Bull 5) Champions 6) The Hustler 7) Follow the
Sun 8) Somebody Up There Likes Me

Q3 1) American Football 2) Rugby 3) Cricket 4) Athletics
(relay) 5) Australian Rules Football 6) Baseball 7) Diving
8) Cycling

Q4 1) They both failed an Olympic Games drugs test and
were banned 2) They are Olympic gold medallists who had
polio as children 3) Both bit their opponents
4) They both won gold medals and broke the world record
in one go (Beamon - long jump, Edwards - triple jump)
5) They are both types of fencing swords 6) Both are
Canadians who turned British 7) Both are famous for
running barefoot 8) Both are terms used to describe
left-handers

Q5 American Football

Q6 1) Curling 2) Croquet or polo 3) Rock climbing
4) Sled dog racing 5) Snooker 6) Yachting 7) Chess
8) Canoeing

Q7 1) Six 2) Three 3) Seven in the water, 11 in the squad
4) None 5) 18 6) 60 7) 200 8) Four

Q8 1) 16 lb or 7.26 kg 2) $3 million (£1.875 million)
3) £23,000 ($36,800) 4) £20 a week 5) 160 lb or 72.6 kg
6) Nine 7) 420 lb or 190 kg 8) 16 lb or 7.26 kg

Q9 1) Parallel bars 2) High jump 3) Double sculls 4) Foil

5) 200 metre butterfly 6) Two man bobsled
7) Hammer throw 8) Figure skating

Q10 Baseball

Q11 1) Honolulu blue and silver 2) Black 3) White
4) Orange 5) Black, blue, red, green, yellow 6) Yellow
7) White with red polka dots 8) White with red tags

Q12 1) Tsuneyuki 2) Ed 3) Earvin 4) George Herman
5) Frank 6) Ray 7) James 8) Keijo

Q13 1) Golf 2) Soccer 3) Ballooning 4) Motor racing
5) Cricket 6) Polo 7) Tennis 8) Bridge

Q14 1) Golf 2) Rugby Union 3) Soccer 4) Ice Hockey
5) Croquet 6) Yachting 7) American Football 8) Boxing

Q15 1) World Fly Fishing Championships 2) Men's
Singles Badminton World Championships 3) Formula One
Grand Prix races 4) The Derby 5) Tug of War World
Championships 6) Doubles Beach Volleyball World
Championships 7) The Cross Country World
Championships 8) ABC Tenpin Bowling Championships

Q16 In a racing car

Q17 1) Anthony Nesty 2) Nancy Lieberman 3) Eva
Klobukowska 4) Boris Becker 5) Martina Navratilova
6) Matthew Webb 7) Bobby Fischer 8) Steve Redgrave

Q18 1) Jesse Owens 2) Jack Nicklaus 3) Florence
Griffith Joyner 4) Franz Beckenbauer 5) William Perry
6) Froilan Gonzalez 7) Joe Namath 8) Ilie Nastase

Solutions

Q19 1) The Japanese art of swordsmanship
2) A French game played with boules **3)** A court game, with glove or basket and a ball **4)** A court handball game **5)** A two car or bike race over a quarter of a mile (402.3 metres) **6)** A 15-a-side stick and ball game from Ireland **7)** A Korean martial art **8)** An 11-a-side ice hockey game with a ball, not a puck

Q20 1) 13.64 km (8.48 miles) **2)** 25 metre (78 ft 2.5 in)
3) 1 mile and 4 furlongs **4)** 29 ft 2.5 in (8.9 metres)
5) 300 yards (274 metres) **6)** 12 years **7)** 25 seconds
8) 4 miles 374 yards (6,779 metres)

Q21 1) 1980 **2)** 1970 **3)** 1969 **4)** 1954 **5)** 1960 **6)** 1987
7) 1972 **8)** 1954

Q22 1) Cricket **2)** Cycling (Tour de France)
3) Greyhound Racing **4)** Darts **5)** Soccer **6)** Gliding
7) Ice Hockey **8)** Handball

Q23 1) National Basketball Association Most Valuable Player **2)** Marylebone Cricket Club **3)** International Olympic Committee **4)** Confédération Internationale de la Peche Sportive **5)** United States National Lawn Tennis Association **6)** British Boxing Board of Control
7) International Ice Hockey Federation **8)** Fédération Internationale de l'Automobile

Q24 1) Basketball **2)** Croquet **3)** Lacrosse **4)** Tennis
5) Ice Hockey **6)** Golf **7)** Volleyball **8)** Chess

Q25 1) Dean Lukin **2)** Tom Finney **3)** Peter Denning

Solutions

4) Nigel Mansell **5)** Kip Keino **6)** Lasse Viren **7)** Horace Ashenfelter **8)** Johnny Weismuller (Tarzan)

Q26 **1)** O J Simpson **2)** Michael Jordan **3)** Vijay Armritraj **4)** Harold Sakata **5)** Bruce Lee **6)** Bruce Jenner **7)** Muhammad Ali **8)** Clarence 'Buster' Crabbe

Q27 Golf courses

Q28 **1)** Both male **2)** Both female **3)** Male and female (respectively) **4)** Both female **5)** Female and male **6)** Male and female **7)** Female and male **8)** Male and female

Q29 **1)** Sergi Bubka **2)** Bjorn Borg **3)** Severiano Ballesteros **4)** Donald Budge **5)** Donovan Bailey **6)** Maria Bueno **7)** Bonnie Blair **8)** Abebe Bikila

Q30 **1)** Michael Jordan **2)** Boris Becker **3)** Nadia Comaneci **4)** Lee Trevino **5)** Kip Keino **6)** Diego Maradona **7)** Evander Holyfield **8)** Walter Payton

Q31 They are all former Formula One race tracks

Q32 **1)** Cricket **2)** Golf **3)** Baseball **4)** Curling **5)** Archery **6)** Bowls **7)** Canoeing **8)** Karate

Q33 **1)** 10 ft (3.05 metres) **2)** 5 ft (1.525 metres) **3)** 3 ft (0.91 metres) **4)** 8 ft (2.44 metres) **5)** 10 in (0.27 metre) **6)** 10 ft (3.05 metres) **7)** 10 metres (32 ft 8 in) **8)** 6 in (0.15 metre)

Q34 **1)** 46 **2)** 17 **3)** 20 **4)** 18 **5)** 11 **6)** 70 **7)** 16 **8)** 17

Q35 **1)** They both played Tarzan in the movies

Solutions

2) They were both knighted by the Queen **3)** They are both Ryder Cup captains **4)** Both are left-handed **5)** Both scored 2,174 career runs **6)** Both married gold medallists **7)** They both rode Red Rum to Grand National victories **8)** Both are also Indianapolis 500 champions

Q36 Coarse fishing

Q37 **1)** Chile **2)** Jamaica **3)** Brazil **4)** Vietnam **5)** Estonia **6)** Nigeria **7)** Cameroon **8)** Burundi

Q38 **1)** 42,750 **2)** Seven **3)** Seven **4)** Four **5)** None - Russia boycotted the event **6)** Two **7)** 10 **8)** 35,000

Q39 The Tour de France

Q40 **1)** American Football **2)** Bobsleigh **3)** Ice Hockey **4)** Grand Prix Motor Racing **5)** Basketball **6)** Athletics **7)** Golf **8)** Tennis

Q41 Basketball

Q42 **1)** Table Tennis **2)** Cycling **3)** Weightlifting **4)** Bowls **5)** Badminton **6)** Skiing **7)** Ice Hockey **8)** Surfing

Q43 **1)** Swiss **2)** Australian **3)** Romanian **4)** Swedish **5)** Moroccan **6)** Pakistani **7)** New Zealander **8)** American

Q44 **1)** One **2)** Six **3)** 143 miles/230 km **4)** 336 **5)** Five **6)** Four **7)** 1,404 miles/2,258 km **8)** 16

Q45 **1)** Formula One **2)** Cricket **3)** Soccer **4)** Rugby League **5)** Boxing **6)** Basketball **7)** Tennis **8)** Golf

Q46 **1)** Basketball **2)** Swimming (breaststroke)

Solutions

3) Walking 4) Ice Hockey 5) Golf 6) Curling 7) Water Polo 8) American Football

Q47 1) George Orwell 2) Ernest Hemingway
3) John Betjeman 4) P G Wodehouse 5) Charles Dickens
6) Evelyn Waugh 7) William Shakespeare 8) John Clare

Q48 1) Lee Trevino 2) Craig Brown (Scotland soccer manager) 3) Muhammad Ali 4) Bill Vukovich (Indy 500)
5) Yogi Berra 6) Sugar Ray Robinson 7) Billie Jean King
8) John McEnroe

Q49 1) Robert Richards 2) Joseph Guillemot (He finished 2nd) 3) Michael Stensgaard 4) Alfred Gilbert
5) Howard Davis 6) Tommie Smith and John Carlos
7) Anne Ottenbrite (200 metre breaststroke) 8) Baron Pierre de Courbetin

Q50 1) Lloyd (then Mill) 2) Slaney 3) Cawley 4) Joyner
5) King 6) Wockel 7) King 8) Kersee

Q51 1) Dublin, Ireland; Hurling and Gaelic Football 2) Paris, France; Tennis 3) Sheffield, England; Snooker 4) Chicago, USA; Baseball 5) New York, USA; Tennis 6) Melbourne, Australia; Cricket and Australian Rules Football 7) Minnesota, USA; American Football 8) Gloucestershire, England; Horse Trials

Q52 1) 1967 2) 1930 3) 1896 4) 1903 5) 1903
6) 1911 7) 1872 8) 1877

Q53 1) American Football 2) Boxing 3) Soccer
4) Basketball 5) Baseball 6) Ten-pin Bowling 7) Rugby League 8) Ice Hockey

Solutions

Q54 1) Basketball **2)** Ice Hockey **3)** Rugby League
4) Tour de France **5)** Baseball **6)** Australian Rules Football
7) American Football **8)** Soccer

Q55 1) Squash **2)** Soccer **3)** Tennis **4)** Hockey **5)** Golf
6) Cricket **7)** Soccer **8)** Equal

Q56 They have all spent time behind bars
(either in jail or in custody)

Q57 1) Los Angeles, USA **2)** Crooked Stick, Indiana, USA
3) Barcelona, Spain **4)** Valderama, Spain **5)** Miami, USA
6) Chicago, USA **7)** Rome, Italy **8)** Athens, Greece

Q58 1) Josephson sisters **2)** Goran Ivanisevic **3)** Eddie
'the eagle' Edwards **4)** Alain Prost **5)** Ice Hockey
6) Vaulting horse (gymnastics) **7)** Tenpin Bowling
8) Badminton

Q59 1) Goal shooter and goal attack **2)** A judo referee
3) A speed skater **4)** Dennis Rodman **5)** A gymnast
6) Troy Aikman **7)** Chris Boardman **8)** Michael Jordan

Q60 1) Table tennis **2)** Volleyball **3)** Water-skiing
4) Swimming **5)** Squash **6)** Snooker **7)** Wrestling **8)** Sailing

Q61 7) They are father and son, all the other pairs
are brothers

Q62 1) Cocaine **2)** Beta-blockers **3)** Strychnine
4) Alcohol **5)** Stanozolol **6)** Mesocarb **7)** Testosterone
8) Caffeine

Q63 1) Atlanta, USA **2)** Athens, Greece **3)** Japan and

Solutions

Korea 4) London, England 5) Beyond the boundary and behind the bowler's arm 6) Atlanta, USA in 1996 7) Buenos Aires, Argentina 8) Mexico City, Mexico

Q64 1) Soviets won 51-50 2) Argentina won 3-1, after extra time 3) Oakland won 4-0 4) It finished a draw 5) Dallas won 27-17 6) St Kilda won 204-141 7) Sampras won 6-4, 6-3, 6-2 8) New Zealand won 106-4

Q65 1) George Best 2) Michael Andretti 3) Tiger Woods 4) Pete Sampras 5) Donovan Bailey 6) Gail Devers 7) Mary Decker-Slaney 8) Fanie de Villiers

Q66 World Championship Motorcycle Racing

Q67 1) 1992 2) 1974 3) 1979 4) 1962 5) 1996 6) 1980 7) 1986 8) 1970

Q68 1) Paris, France 2) Antwerp, Belgium 3) Los Angeles, USA 4) Melbourne, Australia 5) Rome, Italy 6) Tokyo, Japan 7) Moscow, Russia 8) Barcelona, Spain

Q69 1) Ireland 2) France 3) Hong Kong 4) Canada 5) England 6) Australia 7) USA 8) Scotland

Q70 1) Monaco 2) Imola, Italy 3) Silverstone, UK 4) Hockenheim, Germany 5) Spa-Francorchamps, Belgium 6) Suzuka, Japan 7) Laguna Seca, USA 8) Interlagos, Brazil

Q71 1) USA 2) Bulgaria 3) New Mexico 4) New Zealand 5) France 6) Canada 7) Scotland 8) Australia

Q72 They were all ports of call in the 1997 Whitbread Round the World Race (Yachting)